Learn Bridge in Five Days

Terence Reese

B. T. Batsford Ltd, *London*

First published 1995

© Terence Reese 1995

ISBN 0 7134 7913 2

A CIP catalogue record for this book is available from the British Library.

Typeset by Apsbridge Services Ltd, Nottingham.
Printed by Redwood Books, Trowbridge, Wiltshire
for the publishers,
B. T. Batsford Ltd, 4 Fitzhardinge Street,
London W1H 0AH

A BATSFORD BRIDGE BOOK
Series Editor: Tony Sowter

CONTENTS

FOREWORD

There is a lot to learn in bridge. I have written a number of elementary books, but the intention of this one is to transform a non-bridge player into a bridge player WITHIN 5 DAYS!

You now have a whole 5 days in which to fulfil the ambition of the title. One thing is certain: in a very short while you will bid and play much better than most of your friends. Read and re-read each day's programme until you are certain about everything in it and AT THAT POINT answer the quizzes at the end of the chapter. If any of your answers are wrong – or if you can't think of any likely answer – read the relevant passage once again.

It may strike you that some instructive points are made two or three times in different places. That is quite deliberate. My general objective is to make sure that you pick up the important things. All the rest will come in time.

Terence Reese
July 1995

DAY ONE

1
HOW THE GAME BEGINS

Bridge is a game for four players, two against two. You knew that? Good! From now on, everything will be explained.

Yes, you will need a table and four chairs. Also, a pack of cards, but it is usual to have two packs available. They are used for alternate deals.

Cut and Deal

The first move in a game of rubber bridge (generally a private game, not a tournament) is to cut for partners, unless the partnerships are predetermined, the Smiths against the Browns.

Each of the four players draws a card from a pack that has been spread face downwards across the table. The cards in each of the four suits (no jokers) rank as follows:

$$A K Q J 10 \qquad 9 8 7 6 5 4 3 2$$

The cards from ace to ten are called HONOURS*. The possession of certain honour combinations may at times confer a bonus.

The players who have drawn the highest cards – say a king and a 9 – play against the other two, who have drawn an 8 and a 5.

Suppose there had been two kings in the cut? The suits have a ranking order which never changes:

highest	Spades	(♠)	major suit
	Hearts	(♡)	major suit
	Diamonds	(◇)	minor suit
lowest	Clubs	(♣)	minor suit

---

*When a word has a special meaning in bridge it is printed in capitals on its first appearance, and perhaps later. For the meaning, see Bridge Terms and Phrases on page 83.

Returning to our game, the player who drew the highest card chooses seats and cards. He chooses the blue cards, say, and passes this pack to the player on his left to shuffle. It will help to describe the four players thus:

North

West 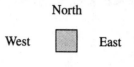 East

South

These descriptions are not used at the table, but they are universal in books and diagrams.

East will cut the pack for South to deal, and North will take charge of the red pack. South will deal the cards one by one to West, then North, and so on. When the deal is completed the players will pick up their cards and (presumably) sort them into suits.

We are ready to begin.

Bidding Procedure

Each of the four players, starting with South, will make a CALL, which may be a PASS, a BID, or (in some circumstances) a DOUBLE or REDOUBLE. The bidding will continue until a call is followed by three passes. One of the four players will be the DECLARER. He will contract to make as many TRICKS as he can (with some regard to safety).

Declarer and Dummy

We are not going to describe the PLAY in any detail at this point; just sufficiently for you to understand the purpose of the bidding.

West, on the declarer's left, will make the OPENING LEAD, placing one card face up in the centre of the table. North will then display the DUMMY, because when play begins the declarer will be in charge of both hands. In most written diagrams the cards are displayed horizontally, but in the actual game they will be vertical, like this:

<pre>
10   K   A   6
 2   8   K   4
      3   7
      2   4
           3
</pre>

Most hands, as a result of the bidding, will be played with a particular suit as TRUMPS. When the dummy is displayed, this suit should be placed on the player's right. For the rest, or in a NO TRUMP contract, there is no prescribed order, but it is normal to alternate the black and red suits.

South will detach a card from dummy, of the same suit as West's opening lead if possible. East (if not VOID) will also follow suit, and so will South. The four cards will form a TRICK. The highest card of the suit led will win the trick, except that a trump will always win against a PLAIN card.

If declarer has won the first trick he or his partner will gather the four cards and lay them face down in front of himself. If a defender has won, his partner will gather the trick and lay it on his side of the table. Subsequent tricks won by either side will be placed aslant the first. The number of tricks won by either side must always be clear. The player who has just won a trick leads to the next trick. At the end of the hand the pack that has been shuffled by North is passed to South, who will cut for West to deal.

Some Bidding Sequences

We are going to look at some typical bidding sequences. Meanwhile, the meaning of some very familiar concepts will be explained.

	South	West	North	East
1.	Pass	Pass	Pass	Pass

On this occasion, comparatively rare, not one of the four players has judged his hand to be worth an opening bid. They have all passed. Some players would say 'No bid', some would say 'Pass'.

	South	West	North	East
2.	Pass	1NT	Pass	Pass
	Pass			

West's 1NT, which stands for ONE NO TRUMP, is for the moment an undertaking to win seven tricks of the thirteen. This bid would imply that he held a strong balanced hand. As 1NT is followed by three passes, the hand will be played in that contract.

3.	South	West	North	East
	Pass	Pass	1NT	Pass
	3NT	Pass	Pass	Pass

This time North has opened and South has given him a RAISE to 3NT. This means that the side has contracted to make at least nine tricks (6+3). 3NT is a GAME contract. The first side to win two games wins the RUBBER, which carries with it a substantial bonus.

To make a game you need to score 100 points 'below the line', which means that the score for contracts made is entered below the thick line across the centre of the scoresheet. This is how the score runs:

A score of 100 equals game.

At No Trumps, the first trick (above 6) counts 40, subsequent tricks 30, so that 3NT is a game contract.

Spades and hearts, the major suits, count 30 for each trick, so that Four Spades and Four Hearts are game contracts.

Diamonds and clubs, the minor suits, count 20 for each trick, so that Five Diamonds and Five Clubs are game contracts.

This is not the end of the scoring, but it shows how points are recorded below the line.

4.	South	West	North	East
	Pass	1♡	Pass	1♠
	Pass	2♡	Pass	Pass
	Pass			

This time West opens in second position and becomes declarer in a PARTSCORE contract. To score a game it is not necessary to record 100 points on a single hand. If West makes his contract of Two Hearts he will enter 60 below (30 a trick, remember); OVERTRICKS, also 30 each, will be entered above the line. If on the next hand, or on any hand before someone has made a game, he scores 40 or more below the line, he will have made game.

5.	South	West	North	East
	1♠	2◇	2♠	3◇
	Pass	Pass	Pass	

This is a 'contested auction', inasmuch as both sides have entered the auction, though at a modest level. West's Two Diamonds is an OVERCALL.

It is time now to introduce a new feature – a PENALTY DOUBLE.

6.	South	West	North	East
	1♠	Pass	2♠(i)	Pass
	2NT(ii)	Pass	3♠(iii)	Pass
	4♠(iv)	Pass	Pass	Double(v)
	Pass	Pass	Pass	

(i)   A limited, possibly weak, raise of partner's suit.

(ii) South, with a strong hand, presses on.

(iii) North has various choices at this moment. He could pass, raise to 3NT, bid a discouraging Three Spades, or jump to Four Spades.

(iv) He does not respect his partner's SIGN-OFF. It was slightly inconsistent on South's part to make a game try and then bid again.

(v)   East 'doesn't like the bidding', or perhaps his hand contains a feature (probably four trumps) that he knows will embarrass the opposition.

The double will raise the stakes whether the contract is made or not. It is possible for North or South to REDOUBLE, but we won't go into that for the moment.

7.	South	West	North	East
	1◇	Pass	1♠	Pass
	2♡	Pass	4♡	Pass
	6♡	Pass	Pass	Pass

This is our first encounter with SLAM bidding. Any contract at the Six or Seven level is a slam contract which if successful will bring in a substantial bonus. Six Hearts (12 tricks) is a small slam. Seven Hearts (13 tricks), a grand slam, is quite rare.

8.	South	West	North	East
	1♡	1♠	2♡	2♠
	4♡	Pass	Pass	4♠
	Dble	Pass	Pass	Pass

It looks as though East is SACRIFICING. He expects to go one or two down in Four Spades, but that will still be a good result if North-South were going to make Four Hearts. Two down doubled costs less than the value of a game.

Vulnerability

There is one element in the scoring which I have not mentioned. A side that has made a game is said to be VULNERABLE. This has an important effect, not so much on constructive bidding as on competitive deals where both sides are in the auction. Both the rewards and the penalties are increased. For example, two down doubled, not vulnerable, costs 300; two down doubled and vulnerable costs 500.

Partly because of the vulnerability factor, opening bids at the Three level are often sacrificial in intent. So you will often encounter a sequence like this:

9.	South	West	North	East
	3◇	3♡	5◇	Pass
	Pass	Pass		

South, not vulnerable, opens Three Diamonds, a relatively weak call. West comes in with Three Hearts and North jumps to Five Diamonds. This may be primarily a defensive move, but on this occasion neither opponent is prepared to double.

Check-back

On Day Two we shall be looking at various possible developments in the bidding. Meanwhile, you may like to be sure that you have taken in all the main points that have been made so far. You should be able to say:

How to cut for partners

Who deals

What happens to the second pack

Who makes the first call

What is the ranking order of the suits

How many tricks are needed for game at no trumps and in the various suits

How many tricks are needed for a small slam, and how many for a grand slam

When a side becomes vulnerable

Who becomes declarer

Who makes the opening lead

How the dummy is arranged

Who collects the declarer's winning tricks

Who collects the defenders' winning tricks

How the tricks are stacked

If you have been able to answer the majority of these questions without looking back you have made an excellent start. And if some of the answers elude you, there is plenty of time to read again.

DAY TWO

2
SIMPLE BIDDING

On Day One you had a picture of the two main elements in the game – bidding and play. Today we look in more detail at the bidding.

Point Count

If you have ever listened to bridge players talking to one another you will have heard remarks along the lines of 'I had 18 points, my partner was marked with 6 or 7, so I ...'.

This is the 'point count', a simple way of expressing high cards, which are valued on this scale:

Ace	equals	4 points
King	equals	3 points
Queen	equals	2 points
Jack	equals	1 point

For bidding on balanced hands (no singleton at any rate) these are rough standards:

A combined 23 or 24 points (out of 40) will usually produce about 8 tricks.

A combined 25 points should put you in the game zone (9 tricks at no trumps).

Most slam contracts (12 or 13 tricks) depend on possessing long suits and adequate controls; when both hands are balanced you may expect to be in the slam zone with a combined total of 33.

But it is not too early to say that you will never be a player if you hang your hat on the number of points you hold.

1NT Opening

There are two main styles of no trump opening. On the one side there is the so-called WEAK NO TRUMP, generally 12-14; on the other side the STRONG NO TRUMP, 15-17. It is also quite common to play a weak no trump when not vulnerable and a strong no trump when vulnerable.

A weak, or variable, no trump is common in the tournament world, where the scoring is different. At rubber bridge it is sensible to play strong throughout. These are some hands on which you might think of opening 1NT:

♠ Q8
♡ KJ954
◇ A104
♣ KQ5

15 points

The five-card suit, even a major, is no bar to opening 1NT. When you can express your hand with a single call, by all means do so.

♠ A1083
♡ 52
◇ KQ104
♣ AK6

16 points

To open 1NT would not be a crime, but the low DOUBLETON is a bad holding, the more so as the opening lead from West will be through any strength that North may hold in the suit. The natural opening for South is One Diamond, preferring this to the moderate four-card major.

♠ A108
♡ K742
◇ A62
♣ Q93

13 points

You have a balanced hand but only 13 points, below strength for an opening 1NT. Open One Club, intending to raise a response of One Heart to Two Hearts and to rebid 1NT over One Diamond or One Spade.

Notice that by opening the bidding with One Club albeit with only a three card suit you keep the bidding at a low level. If you opened the bidding with One Heart, a response of Two Clubs or Two Diamonds would force you to reach at least 2NT.

Responding to a 1NT Opening

On a balanced hand it is fairly easy to judge the first response. Partner has opened 1NT, 15-17, and you hold:

♠ Q965
♡ AJ8
◇ J74
♣ J85

9 points

Adding your 9 points to partner's minimum of 15, you are well worth 2NT. You hold honours in every suit and are not far from a raise to 3NT. It is quite correct to be in game contracts which may be odds against.

♠ Q10
♡ Q63
◇ 94
♣ K108742

7 points

This is an awkward type of hand. Everything is likely to depend on how the clubs go. Either take a chance with 3NT or pass 1NT. Two Clubs (as we shall see in a moment) would be conventional; it would have a special meaning, unrelated to clubs.

♠ AK
♡ J74
◇ 106542
♣ 974

8 points

You have enough, in terms of the point count, for a raise to 2NT, but the doubleton AK is a poor feature, unlikely to pull its weight in terms of points. Two Diamonds might play well, but the sensible action is to pass 1NT.

Two Club Response to 1NT

There is a conventional response to 1NT – Two Clubs, generally known as STAYMAN, after the American player, Sam Stayman. This response asks partner to name a four-card major if he has one; if not, to bid Two Diamonds.

The best time – the only time, some would say – for a Stayman response is when you hold four cards in one or both majors and a singleton elsewhere, a hand such as:

♠ 7
♡ K1082
◇ J873
♣ A652

You can bid Two Clubs here because partner may hold four hearts, which should lead to a game in hearts. Much more often he will bid Two Spades, which you will transfer to 2NT. If his response to Two Clubs is Two Diamonds (no four-card major) you can pass; Five of a minor might be on, but the bidding to get there would be tricky.

I should add that there is no imperial necessity to play Stayman. Sometimes it works well, more often it gives away information unnecessarily. But when you move into the wider world, especially the club world, you will find that knowledge of the convention will be expected.

Responses of 2◇, 2♡ and 2♠

These responses are normally played as weak, not encouraging any further action by the no trump opener. It is common to respond at the Two level on quite bad hands, such as six to the queen and a 'bust'.

Opening 2NT

The usual standard for a 2NT opening is 20-22 points. Any response to this at the level of three is forcing. If you have agreed to play Stayman over 1NT it will be assumed that you play the same style over 2NT. A small difference is that 2NT – 3♣ – 3NT will imply that the opener's only four-card suit is clubs. (The sequence 1NT – 2♣ – 2NT does not exist, because the responder might be quite weak.)

Opening 3NT

You might think that an opening 3NT would signify a somewhat stronger hand than an opening 2NT, but that is not so. With a very strong balanced hand you can open Two Clubs (see next section) and rebid in no trumps. Thus an immediate 3NT carries a different meaning. A sensible way to treat the bid is to let it suggest a hand with a long minor suit that might play well in 3NT, something like

♠ Kx
♡ Ax
◇ Jxx
♣ AKQ10xx

This is a matter on which you need to have an understanding with your partner, because the opening 3NT is differently interpreted in different bidding systems.

Opening Two Clubs

A Two Club opening provides a home for any big hand that contains at least five HONOUR TRICKS (also called Quick Tricks). This is the accepted standard for quick tricks:

AK	2
AQ	$1^1/2$
KQJ	1 to $1^1/2$
Ace	1
KQ	1
King	$^1/2$

Quite an aristocratic selection, as you see. Holdings such as QJ10 are useful, of course, but the object of giving points to the top cards only is that this enables the partners to judge whether they have sufficient *controls* for a slam. If you add up the honour tricks in all four hands you will find that the total will always be around $8^1/2$; if you can judge that you and your partner hold upwards of 7 honour tricks you will be in the slam zone.

The weakness response to Two Clubs is Two Diamonds. You may give a positive response when you hold $1^1/2$ tricks or more, but there is no obligation to do so if this would take you to an uncomfortable level.

We will look first at hands on which you would open Two Clubs.

♠ KQ108
♡ AK5
◊ AQ
♣ AQ42

24 points, balanced; open Two Clubs and rebid 2NT, not forcing. Partner may pass with less than 3 points. True, you might play in 2NT with 26 points between you, but the fact that almost all of these were in the same hand would make the play difficult.

♠ KQ9
♡ A10
◊ AKQ108
♣ AQJ

25 points and a good suit; open Two Clubs and rebid 3NT.

♠ 7
♡ AKJ1075
◊ AKQ8
♣ A5

'Only' 21 points, but 5 honour tricks and a powerful hand, which you will never be afraid to play in Four Hearts. Open Two Clubs.

Responding to Two Clubs is not difficult. Most of the time you will be giving the negative response of Two Diamonds. When you hold a few good cards you will have the choice whether or not to give a 'positive'. These are a couple of borderline hands after partner has opened Two Clubs:

(a) ♠ KQ10863
     ♡ 5
     ◊ Q642
     ♣ 93

On (a) no harm could come from showing the good spades.

(b)   ♠ 743
     ♡ 9
     ◊ K832
     ♣ A7642

On (b) you have the technical requirements for Three Clubs and no-one could say it was wrong to bid this. Partner will rebid Three Hearts, no doubt; then you will bid 3NT and the next move will be up to him.

Opening Two Bids

What about opening bids of Two Diamonds, Two Hearts and Two Spades? There are different ways of treating these calls: you can play them as forcing for one round, strong but not forcing, or weak, such as QJ10xxx and a side ace or king. There may be tactical advantages in the weak Two bid, which is common in the tournament world, but when building a system it is wise to fill in the gaps, so that there will be an answer for any type of hand you pick up. The best way to fill any gap in this area is to play what are known as Acol Two bids, forcing for one round. These will be powerful hands that are short of the five quick tricks needed for an opening Two Clubs, such as:

(a)   ♠ AQJ963
     ♡ KQ1054
     ◊ A2
     ♣ –

On hand (a) you wouldn't like to open One Spade, be left there, and find that partner had a singleton spade and good support for hearts. Open Two Spades, therefore, and over the weakness response of 2NT bid Three Hearts. You are not committed to game.

(b)   ♠ 83
     ♡ AKJ964
     ◊ KJ
     ♣ AK10

On (b) you would open Two Hearts and rebid Three Hearts, again not forcing.

Opening Three Bids

These present few problems. They are PRE-EMPTIVE, meaning that your ambition is to buy the contract before your opponents can get together. Say that in first position you hold:

♠ KJ87542
♡ 6
◇ Q82
♣ 103

An opening Three Spades will surely create a problem for the opposition. If you are doubled and lose 300 or 500 it won't be a tragedy, as you will be saving at least a game, quite possibly a slam.

When vulnerable you need to be somewhat stronger in playing tricks, because if you are doubled and go three down you will lose 800 points. Worse still, four down would cost you 1100. Neither of these would be a bargain unless you were saving against a slam which the enemy would be sure to bid and make.

Opening Four Bids

These, too, are pre-emptive in character, but they need to be quite a bit stronger because the opponents are much more likely to double the game call. There is another temptation – to open with a bid of Four when you are much too strong for that. In first or second hand it is unwise to pre-empt when you hold more than three honour tricks. In third or fourth position you may vary the pre-empt, because you won't be afraid of missing a slam when your partner has already passed.

Review of Opening Bids

If the contents of this chapter were new to you, there has been a lot to learn; but don't be depressed, because once you have played a little the values attached to the various calls will require no effort of memory at all. For the moment, you may like a summary of the opening bids that have been recommended.

Opening bids of One of a suit
These were noted on day one. One of a suit has a wide range, roughly from 11 points to 20.

Opening 1NT
At any score, and in any position at the table, 15-17 points, balanced.

Opening Two Clubs
The big bid, forcing to game except in the sequence 2♣ – 2◊ – 2NT.

Opening Two Diamonds, Two Hearts and Two Spades
Forcing for one round, with 2NT the negative response.

Opening 2NT
20-22 in any position.

Opening Three bids
Weak in the first three positions, may be stronger in fourth.

Opening 3NT
A promising hand, containing a long, strong minor suit.

Opening Four bids
Pre-emptive, but may be stronger in third or fourth position.

Responses to Opening Bids of One

We turn now to an important call – the first response when partner has opened with a bid of One of a suit.

The response on minimum hands
It is usual to keep the bidding open on 6 points. On less than that you may respond when you hold either support for partner's suit or a fair suit of your own which you can bid at the range of One.

Partner has opened One Heart and you hold:

$$\text{(a)} \quad \spadesuit\ 75$$
$$\heartsuit\ \text{J863}$$
$$\diamondsuit\ \text{K42}$$
$$\clubsuit\ \text{10853}$$

On (a) it is in order to respond Two Hearts. It is a sub-minimum raise, but no matter; you will be stealing some bidding space from the opposition. In particular, neither opponent will be able to contest with One Spade. Occasionally, too, partner will go to Four Hearts and make it.

$$\text{(b)} \quad \spadesuit\ \text{A9743}$$
$$\heartsuit\ 4$$
$$\diamondsuit\ \text{J742}$$
$$\clubsuit\ 863$$

On (b) it wouldn't be a crime to pass One Heart, and you might be glad of it later, but most players would respond One Spade.

The response of 1NT
This is the standard response when you hold limited support for partner, about 6 to 9 points, and no suit you are anxious to call. Partner has opened One Diamond and you hold:

$$\text{(c)} \quad \spadesuit\ \text{Q74}$$
$$\heartsuit\ \text{J103}$$
$$\diamondsuit\ \text{Q862}$$
$$\clubsuit\ \text{A85}$$

On (c) a response of 1NT would give a better picture than Two Diamonds.

$$\text{(d)} \quad \spadesuit\ \text{Q854}$$
$$\heartsuit\ 742$$
$$\diamondsuit\ \text{Q103}$$
$$\clubsuit\ \text{A842}$$

On (d) the balanced shape suggests 1NT rather than One Spade. Some players would say that they make it a rule to respond on a four-card major. It is silly to make a rule about anything at this game.

Raising partner's suit

This is a matter of playing tricks, not of high-card strength. In general, when you can do so you should support a major suit. Partner opens One Spade and you hold:

(e) ♠ K1054
♡ 62
◇ AQ952
♣ 108

On (e) you have a natural raise to Three Spades. This is not forcing, though it is seldom passed.

(f) ♠ Q953
♡ –
◇ A87
♣ K107542

Hand (f) is what we call a 'shape' hand. Raise to Four Spades rather than dally with the clubs.

Suit responses on medium hands

A suit response at the level of One has a very wide range. At the level of Two responder is expected to hold fair values, usually upwards of 10 points to bid a new suit. Partner opens One Heart and you hold:

(g) ♠ A974
♡ 5
◇ KJ862
♣ 1053

On (g) you would respond One Spade, because you are under strength for Two Diamonds.

(h) ♠ 85
♡ 42
◇ AQ7432
♣ Q65

Hand (h) is an awkward type because 1NT doesn't look attractive, and again you are under strength for Two Diamonds. Both responses would have their supporters.

With two-suited hands, it is usual to bid 'upwards' when you are 4-4; with 5-5 bid the higher suit first. Partner has opened One Club and you hold:

(i) ♠ KJ82
     ♡ A1075
     ◊ Q4
     ♣ 632

On (i) respond One Heart. If partner then by-passes spades you will be under no obligation to introduce that suit.

(j) ♠ J4
     ♡ Q10852
     ◊ AJ973
     ♣ 9

On (j) respond One Heart and show the diamonds on the next round.

Suit responses on strong hands
The modern fashion is to respond at the One level on quite strong hands. Partner opens One Diamond and you hold:

(k) ♠ AJ85
     ♡ J2
     ◊ AQ6
     ♣ KJ53

On (k) you can be sure of game, certainly, but you may need time to find your best spot. Respond simply One Spade and take strong action on the next round. A bid of a new suit will always be forcing.

(l) ♠ A5
     ♡ AQJ962
     ◊ A107
     ♣ 84

On (l) it is sensible to FORCE with Two Hearts, though many players would respond One Heart and have to invent a call on the next round to be sure of keeping the ship afloat.

Responses of 2NT and 3NT

No problem here; respond 2NT on balanced hands in the 11-12 range, 3NT with 13-15.

> (m) ♠ Q852
> ♡ K95
> ◇ A1052
> ♣ Q3

On (m) you would raise an opening One Spade to Three Spades; respond 2NT to any other opening.

> (n) ♠ KJ5
> ♡ A108
> ◇ QJ6
> ♣ K652

On (n) respond 3NT to any suit bid of One. This is not an easy response to manage, however, so don't be keen on it unless you hold the rather non-co-operative 4-3-3-3 distribution.

There has been a lot to learn in this chapter. Test yourself on these quizzes to see if you have picked up the main points.

Quiz No. 1

1. On average, how many points will be enough for a side to make 2NT?

2. How many points to make 3NT?

3. How many points are required for a weak no trump?

4. How many for a strong no trump?

5. How many points are there in the pack?

6. What action do you take on a balanced hand which is not good enough for an opening 1NT?

Quiz No. 2

7. Partner has opened 1NT. How many points do you need on average for a raise to 2NT?

8. What is meant by the Stayman convention?

9. What is the general sense of responding Two Diamonds, Two Hearts or Two Spades to 1NT?

10. How many points do you need to open 2NT?

11. What is the meaning of Three Clubs in response to 2NT?

Quiz No. 3

12. How many honour tricks do you need for an opening Two Clubs?

13. What is needed for a positive response?

14. How many points does the sequence 2♣ – 2◊ – 2NT suggest?

15. What is meant by an Acol Two bid?

16. To what level is an opening Two bid forcing?

17. What is the meaning of an opening Three bid?

Quiz No. 4

18. Over partner's opening bid of One, how many points does a response of 1NT suggest?

19. How many points do you need for a raise of opener's major suit to the Two level?

20. How many points do you need for a response in a new suit at the Two level to partner's opening One of a suit bid?

21. Which of touching four-card suits do you bid first when responding to an opening bid?

22. What is the usual standard for a response of 2NT to an opening bid of One?

Answers to Quiz No. 1

1. 23 to 24.

2. 25 upwards.

3. 12 to 14.

4. 15 to 17.

5. 40.

6. Open your longer minor suit, One Club if they are 3-3.

Answers to Quiz No. 2

7. 8 to 9.

8. Playing the convention, Two Clubs over 1NT asks the opener to name a four-card major, and otherwise to bid Two Diamonds.

9. They are all weakness responses; opener is expected to pass.

10. 20 to 22.

11. If you are playing Stayman, it will have a similar sense to Two Clubs over 1NT; if not, it will be natural and forcing.

Answers to Quiz No. 3

12. Normally 5, but this doesn't mean that you have to open Two Clubs with 5 honour tricks.

13. In general, $1\frac{1}{2}$ honour tricks, but this is not a strict requirement.

14. 23 to 24.

15. A powerful hand, normally in the range of $3\frac{1}{2}$ to 5 honour tricks.

16. Only as far as opener's rebid over the negative 2NT response.

17. A weak shut-out, called a pre-empt, usually a seven-card suit and at most $1\frac{1}{2}$ honour tricks.

Answers to Quiz No. 4

18. 6 to 9; more like 8 to 10 over One Club.

19. This was a horrible trap! Points don't come into it. Distribution and tactics are more important.

20. The normal standard is 10 points, but sometimes one has to make the bid on less.

21. On hands of limited strength it is better to respond in the lower suit. If you expect to bid both suits, then start with the higher.

22. 11 to 12 points.

DAY THREE

3
DECLARER'S PLAY

The declarer plays the cards from dummy and from his own hand. It may surprise you that as a rule this is easier than playing the defence. As declarer you can see two hands in combination and can form a plan more surely than the defenders, who at the start of play see only their own cards and those of dummy.

Forming a Plan at No Trumps

You are in 3NT and must aim to take nine tricks. West leads the 3 of spades and you see:

```
              ♠ 95
              ♡ AJ92
              ◊ K84
              ♣ J873
                      N
♠3 led          W         E
                      S
              ♠ KQ4
              ♡ K105
              ◊ AQ105
              ♣ A62
```

South	West	North	East
1◊	Pass	1♡	Pass
2NT	Pass	3NT	Pass
Pass	Pass		

Sitting South, you were too strong for 1NT, so you began with One Diamond. North responded One Heart, you jumped to 2NT and he raised to 3NT. Simple enough; every pair in the room, as we say in the tournament world, would be in 3NT with the combined 27 points.

However, the contract is not laydown. East plays the jack of spades on the first trick and it is advisable to win with the – well, which? The king, certainly, because if West has led from something like A10xxx he won't be sure who holds the queen.

You have only seven tricks on top – one spade, two hearts, three diamonds and one club. The natural play is to cross to the ace of hearts and return a heart to the 10. If West is able to win with the queen he will have various options. It is quite likely that he will play a neutral game, returning a heart.

South can see eight tricks now and his chance for the contract is likely to depend on making four tricks in diamonds. His best line is to play ace and king of diamonds, cash the thirteenth heart, and lead a diamond towards the Q10. If he has to guess at this point he will probably FINESSE the 10, because West is marked with much longer spades than his partner.

Many no trump contracts depend on the art of being able to go from hand to hand at the right moment. Consider South's situation on the following deal:

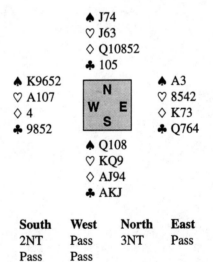

```
                    ♠ J74
                    ♡ J63
                    ◇ Q10852
                    ♣ 105
    ♠ K9652          ┌─────────┐          ♠ A3
    ♡ A107           │    N    │          ♡ 8542
    ◇ 4              │  W   E  │          ◇ K73
    ♣ 9852           │    S    │          ♣ Q764
                    └─────────┘
                    ♠ Q108
                    ♡ KQ9
                    ◇ AJ94
                    ♣ AKJ
```

South	West	North	East
2NT	Pass	3NT	Pass
Pass	Pass		

West leads the 5 of spades to the ace, and when a spade is returned South's queen is allowed to hold. Good play by West, because South has no quick entry to dummy. He may try a low heart, but West will certainly go in with the ace and cash three more spades for one down.

South might have played the 10 of spades at trick two, but then West would have won with the king and returned a third spade, putting South in the same position as before.

Have you missed the point – as many players would at the table? On the very first trick, South must UNBLOCK the queen of spades; then dummy's jack of spades will always be an ENTRY. When in dummy South will run the 10 of diamonds; he will return to dummy on the fourth round of the suit, cash the fifth diamond, and if necessary finesse the jack of clubs for his ninth trick.

Another common strategy in no trump contracts is to let the enemy do the work.

♠ A1087
♡ J106
◇ KJ5
♣ J96

♠ K62		♠ 543
♡ Q852	N	♡ A73
◇ Q632	W E	◇ 98
♣ A4	S	♣ K10732

♠ QJ9
♡ K94
◇ A1074
♣ Q85

South	West	North	East
1◇	Pass	1♠	Pass
1NT	Pass	2NT	Pass
Pass	Pass		

West's lead of the 2 of hearts runs to the ace and East returns the 7. Not much would be gained by holding up at this point; South forms a different plan, deciding to keep the 9 of hearts as an EXIT card.

He wins with the king of hearts, therefore, and takes the spade finesse. When this wins he plays off four rounds of the suit, East discarding a club, South a diamond and West a diamond. At this point South exits with a heart. After West has taken the queen and the 8, the ENDGAME will look like this:

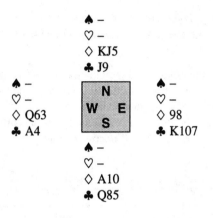

West will probably exit with a low diamond. South will cash the 10 and the ace, then advance a low club; whether West plays high or low, South will make the last trick.

This was not such an easy hand, so don't be too proud to make a copy and tick off the cards from the beginning. South had five top losers – three hearts and two clubs – and managed to avoid any additional hazard such as a finesse in diamonds or clubs.

The Play of Suit Combinations

Before passing on to defence we are going to take a look at the way for declarer to play different combinations in a single suit. Suppose that in one suit he holds this combination:

AQ74

K63

Three top tricks; but what chance of finding the suit 3-3 and developing a fourth? It is important to know this kind of thing because it will often determine your play.

According to the mathematicians, the odds against a 3-3 break are about 7 to 4. Many players base their play on that expectation. This is seriously wrong, however. For one thing, unless there is a peculiar break in another suit, the odds shorten every time a card is played. (Suppose, for example, that neither defender has played a card of this suit by the time you reach trick eleven; then the remaining cards in the defending hands *must* be breaking 3-3.) When you hold seven cards in a suit, be at any rate hopeful of a 3-3 break.

With eight cards, KQxxx opposite Axx, expect a 3-2 break unless there is definite evidence to the contrary; in other words, plan the play on the assumption that the suit will provide five tricks.

This is a critical combination:

A105

KJ9632

If you have to play this suit early on, the odds slightly favour a 2-2 break; but if there is any indication that one defender has length in another suit, it will be right to play his partner for Qxx.

This is not the first time we have encountered the very familiar type of play known as a FINESSE. There will be opportunity for one or more finesses on almost every hand you play. Do not imagine, however, that a finesse is in itself a desirable manoeuvre. Players grow old looking for a clever play that will avoid the risk of a finesse.

There are many combinations, nevertheless, where the general plan is to take *two* finesses.

753

Q86 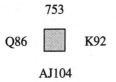 K92

AJ104

When this suit breaks 3-3 and the honours are divided you can establish three winners. You lead from dummy and finesse the jack, losing to West's queen. On the next round you finesse the 10 and so pick up all the remaining tricks.

You may employ the same sort of tactics when your object is to lose not more than two tricks with this kind of combination:

K1095

Q84 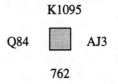 AJ3

762

A finesse of the 9 loses to the jack. On the next round the odds favour a finesse of the 10. This will force the ace, and when the suit breaks 3-3 you will have developed two tricks from your moderate holding.

Safety Plays in a Single Suit

There is an important group of what are known as 'safety plays'. The principle appears in this simple example:

AQ1054

K963

You must begin with the ace or queen, so that you can pick up Jxxx in either hand.

The list of safety plays is a long one. It may be best to take note of one or two general principles.

(a)   J5

Q1073 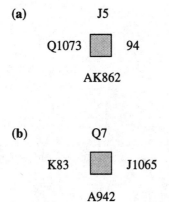 94

AK862

(b)   Q7

K83   J1065

A942

On occasions like this lead towards the unsupported honour.

(c)   AQ753

          K9   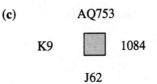   1084

              J62

When you 'cannot afford a cover', as we say, don't waste a high card. The lead of the jack in (c) can only cost a trick – it can never gain, because the defender here will follow the established rule of covering an honour with an honour.

(d)   AJ104

          K7   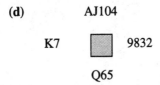   9832

              Q65

On (d), if you are able to lead low from the South hand on each of the first two rounds you will win four tricks.

(e)   A62

          93   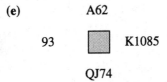   K1085

              QJ74

If with (e) your object is to develop three tricks, the way to begin is to lead towards the QJ74. To lead the queen from hand can never gain.

(f)   AQ763

          J94   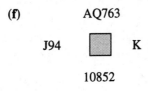   K

              10852

With (f), the only chance for *five* tricks will be to finesse the queen and find West with precisely Kx; but for *four* tricks ace first is the game. There are numerous situations of this kind, where the safety play is to begin with the ace.

The Ruffing Game

We shall be looking next at the declarer's play in a suit (or trump) contract. The trump suit provides many ways of making extra tricks. If you can make a trick with a trump in the 'short' hand you have gained a trick that would not be available at no trumps.

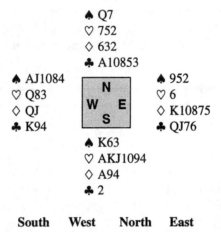

```
                    ♠ Q7
                    ♡ 752
                    ◊ 632
                    ♣ A10853
   ♠ AJ1084       ┌─────────┐      ♠ 952
   ♡ Q83          │    N    │      ♡ 6
   ◊ QJ           │ W     E │      ◊ K10875
   ♣ K94          │    S    │      ♣ QJ76
                  └─────────┘
                    ♠ K63
                    ♡ AKJ1094
                    ◊ A94
                    ♣ 2
```

South	West	North	East
1♡	1♠	Pass	2♠(i)
3♡	Pass	Pass(ii)	Pass

(i)   Although his trumps are moderate, East will expect his partner to hold at least five for his overcall. The raise to Two Spades is not meant to sound strong.

(ii) North has a few cards, but the Qx of a suit the opponents have called is apt to be of no value (though it happens to be on this occasion).

West might have led a spade, but the queen of diamonds turns out a good choice. South would probably hold off the first round and West would follow with the jack. East overtakes with the king and South wins with the ace.

Now South *might* lay down ace and king of hearts. Other things being equal, it is right to draw trumps, but on this occasion it is essential to take the ruff in spades, and no danger threatens. South should lead a low spade to the queen and return a spade, which will be won by West. There is nothing the defence can do now. In due course South will make nine tricks by way of five hearts, a spade, a spade ruff, and the minor suit aces.

It is worth remarking that Three Hearts, bid and made, is a PAR result on this deal. East-West would probably go one down in Three Spades; this would be a fair result for them too.

On many hands declarer won't draw trumps at all. He will play what is called a CROSS-RUFF, making his trumps separately.

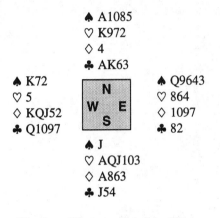

```
                    ♠ A1085
                    ♡ K972
                    ◇ 4
                    ♣ AK63
    ♠ K72                        ♠ Q9643
    ♡ 5           N              ♡ 864
    ◇ KQJ52    W     E           ◇ 1097
    ♣ Q1097       S              ♣ 82
                    ♠ J
                    ♡ AQJ103
                    ◇ A863
                    ♣ J54
```

South	West	North	East
–	–	1♣	Pass
1♡	Pass	3♡	Pass
4◇(i)	Pass	4♠(ii)	Pass
6♡(iii)	Pass	Pass	Pass

(i) After partner has opened the bidding and then jumped, a slam is already likely. One way of looking at it is this: even without the ace of diamonds you would expect Four Hearts to be easy. Four Diamonds is a cuebid. In the present context it indicates a diamond control and interest in a slam.

(ii) North responds with a cuebid above game level, showing that he is quite willing to advance to a slam.

(iii) South requires no further invitation.

West will probably lead the king of diamonds. South sees at once that the hands fit well for a cross-ruff. He wins the ace of diamonds and ruffs a diamond, returns to the queen of hearts and ruffs another diamond. At this point it would be good play to cash the ace and king of clubs. It is standard technique when you are cross-ruffing to cash side winners, to prevent any possibility of these cards being ruffed if you play them later on.

After the ace of spades and a spade ruff South ruffs his fourth diamond. Already the contract is safe, since these are the remaining cards:

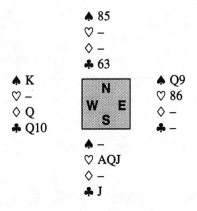

South loses only the last trick, the jack of clubs.

Quite often a trump lead is best for the defence when it is clear that declarer has numerous trumps in both hands. An experienced player might have led a trump on the West cards, despite the powerful holding in diamonds. On this occasion the imaginative lead is not quite enough; South can make five hearts in his own hand, four top winners in the side suits, and three diamond ruffs.

Establishing Side Suits

A very useful function of the trump suit is to aid in the establishment of long side suits.

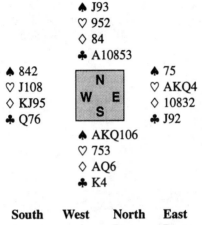

```
                      ♠ J93
                      ♡ 952
                      ◊ 84
                      ♣ A10853
    ♠ 842                           ♠ 75
    ♡ J108            N             ♡ AKQ4
    ◊ KJ95        W       E         ◊ 10832
    ♣ Q76             S             ♣ J92
                      ♠ AKQ106
                      ♡ 753
                      ◊ AQ6
                      ♣ K4
```

South	West	North	East
–	–	Pass	Pass
1♠	Pass	2♠ (i)	Pass
4♠ (ii)	Pass	Pass	Pass

(i)   North hasn't much, and the trump support is indifferent, but it is normal to raise on this type of hand.

(ii) This is borderline, actually. South might have preferred something like Three Diamonds, a TRIAL bid inviting Four Spades.

West leads the jack of hearts and the defenders take three tricks in this suit. Then East leads a low diamond. South has two chances now – the diamond finesse, or to make enough tricks in clubs to provide discards for the losing diamonds.

An important consideration is that East, who passed in second position, has already turned up with AKQ of hearts. This does not exclude his holding the king of diamonds but, as there is a fair chance of setting up tricks in clubs, most players would go up with the ace of diamonds, then play king, ace and another club, ruffing high. Then South can win the third round of trumps in dummy and discard his losing diamonds on winning clubs.

There is another possibility in the deal, which may not have occurred to you. A good player in East's position, after winning three tricks in hearts, might think to himself: 'South is very likely to hold the ace of diamonds. I wonder whether I should lead the thirteenth heart, in the hope of finding my partner with Qx of spades?' It's a thought, certainly, but the play would be a mistake if South had AK of diamonds and no better than Qx in clubs. In that case he might be able to discard the club loser and ruff safely in dummy.

Sometimes one or two ruffs in the dummy will enable the declarer to establish his own side suit.

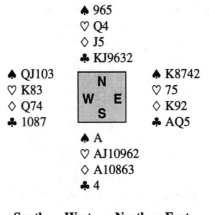

```
              ♠ 965
              ♡ Q4
              ◇ J5
              ♣ KJ9632
♠ QJ103                      ♠ K8742
♡ K83          N             ♡ 75
◇ Q74        W   E           ◇ K92
♣ 1087         S             ♣ AQ5
              ♠ A
              ♡ AJ10962
              ◇ A10863
              ♣ 4
```

South	West	North	East
1♡	Pass	1NT	Pass
2◇	Pass	2♡	Pass
3♡(i)	Pass	4♡(ii)	Pass
Pass	Pass		

(i)   He cannot consider bidding more than this, because partner's values may be in all the wrong places.

(ii)   North knows that his clubs may not be worth much, but the queen of hearts and the jack of diamonds should be useful cards.

West's lead of the queen of spades runs to the ace. South must hope for a reasonable break in diamonds; for the moment there is nothing to do but lead a low diamond. West will play low, because he can be fairly sure that his partner holds one of the top honours. East will head the jack with the king and lead a low heart. South won't let this run because he can see a better chance.

The natural play is to go up with the ace of hearts, cash the ace of diamonds, and ruff a diamond with the queen of hearts. The 3-3 split is good news. South will come to hand with a spade ruff and lead the jack of hearts. He will make his contract now, losing just one heart, one diamond and one club.

Quiz No 5

1. You hold seven cards in a suit; what are the chances of finding a 3-3 break?

2. You hold nine cards in a suit; what are the chances of a 3-1 break?

3. What is a par result?

4. What is a cross-ruff?

5. What is a cuebid?

6. What is a trial bid?

Answers to Quiz No. 5

1. Initially (unless the bidding has supplied a clue of some kind) it is 7 to 4 against a 3-3 break; but the odds soon become shorter as the play proceeds, and the bidding may have supplied a clue.

2. At the beginning of play, slightly less than evens.

3. The best that a side could achieve on a deal; also, a result that represents the best for both sides.

4. A play where a side makes its trumps separately, ruffing in both hands.

5. Usually a bid that indicates a top control, ace or king; it may also indicate a ruffing control, singleton or void.

6. A bid that does not show length in the suit named but invites support for a suit previously bid by the partnership.

DAY FOUR

4
DEFENSIVE PLAY

As we have noted already, the player on the left of the declarer makes his opening lead before the dummy has gone down. This is an important moment in almost every hand. Broadly speaking, these are the main alternatives:

Against a No Trump Contract

The general plan, as a rule, will be to establish the long suits in your (and your partner's) hand before the declarer has begun to establish the long suits his way. The advantage is seen on this type of hand:

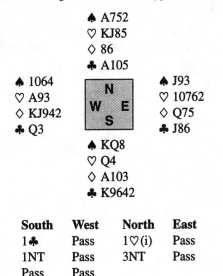

```
                    ♠ A752
                    ♡ KJ85
                    ◇ 86
                    ♣ A105
    ♠ 1064          N          ♠ J93
    ♡ A93       W       E      ♡ 10762
    ◇ KJ942         S          ◇ Q75
    ♣ Q3                       ♣ J86
                    ♠ KQ8
                    ♡ Q4
                    ◇ A103
                    ♣ K9642
```

South	West	North	East
1♣	Pass	1♡(i)	Pass
1NT	Pass	3NT	Pass
Pass	Pass		

(i) With 4-4 in touching suits it is usual to respond the lower suit.

West's lead is not much of a problem. Though it may well cost a trick if partner has no high honour, West should begin with a low diamond. The usual card would be fourth best – in this case, the 4. East plays the queen.

South could win with the ace, but it is generally wrong to part with a winning card so soon. A better plan is to HOLD UP the winner for at least two rounds.

East, naturally, will continue to lead diamonds. On the third round South will have to discard from dummy. He will probably choose a heart.

To have any chance for game, South must aim to develop the clubs without letting West into the lead. He will lead a low club and put in the 10 from dummy. Unlucky! East wins and will surely try a heart. West will be happy to take the ace and cash his two winning diamonds. The defenders have taken six tricks, so South is two down. North-South had enough high cards for game, but the hands didn't fit well; the danger suit was led and the player with the long diamonds had the critical ENTRY CARD, the ace of hearts.

Now, a small digression. People who are new to the game often find it difficult to read a diagram and may be tempted to pick out actual cards and turn them over as they are played. If that is a temptation, resist it. In a very short while you will read the diagram of 52 cards as easily as any headline.

Very often, of course, you won't have a comfortable fourth-best lead from a promising suit. Suppose the bidding by North-South goes like this:

South	North
–	1 ◇
2NT	3NT

Sitting West, you have to find a lead from:

♠ 742
♡ K873
◇ J63
♣ 654

Fourth best from your longest and strongest, the 3 of hearts, is not very appealing. It's a poor suit and you are short of possible entry cards. There is nothing to recommend a diamond lead. As between spades and clubs, where does the balance lie?

Most players, I am sure, would lead a spade, because it is usual to attack a major suit which neither opponent has introduced. Nevertheless, there is a sound argument in favour of a club. You are not going to beat this contract unless your partner has a fair hand, and it should strike you that he did not take the opportunity to overcall at the One level. So his holding in spades cannot be great. But he could hold something like KQ10xx in clubs, with a side ace, and still not care to overcall at the Two level. Thus there is a sound reason for preferring a club lead to a spade. You will have to make decisions of this kind every time you play, so use your brains!

The Lead against a Suit Contract

This is one of the most critical situations in the game. As a defender, you must listen to the bidding and decide where the opponents may have a weakness. Suppose they have bid to game, mentioning only one suit, a sequence such as:

South	North
1♠	3♠
4♠	Pass

Now there may be various possible lines of defence. We are going to look at the following possibilities:

1. The lead from a strong honour combination.

2. An attacking lead.

3. Looking for a ruff.

4. A forcing lead.

5. Safety leads.

1. The lead from a strong honour combination
If you are lucky enough to hold a strong combination in a side suit, this will usually be an obvious choice. You will begin with the top of a sequence, the king from KQJ, the queen from QJ10, and so on.

The lead from an AK holding is always attractive, especially from four cards or more. The traditional lead is the king, though it must be said that many players begin with the ace.

2. An attacking lead

Often there is a choice between a negative lead, such as the top card from three small, and a more adventurous lead such as low from Kxxx or Q10xx. From Axxx, the ace is generally preferred. Leads of this kind are safer when you hold a five-card suit.

3. Looking for a ruff

A singleton is generally a good lead – the more so when you have a likely trump trick, such as Ax or Kxx. Sometimes, your partner will hold the ace of the suit you are leading and will be able to give you an immediate ruff. Even if he cannot win the first trick he may come in later, before the trumps have been drawn.

A low doubleton may be a good lead when you hold a likely winner in the trump suit. After the same bidding sequence as before (1♠-3♠-4♠) you have to lead from:

♠ K53
♡ Q8642
◇ 94
♣ K103

You could lead a low heart, as probably you would against a no trump contract, but now it would not be dynamic. The opponents are likely to hold eight or nine spades between them and to be able to ruff heart leads without any discomfort.

There is not much point in a trump lead either. South will win, cash the ace of trumps, and play on whichever is the stronger of his side suits.

You *might* lead a club and be lucky, finding your partner with QJ8 and establishing two tricks which might not otherwise have been available.

However, the obvious lead is the 9 of diamonds. If your partner holds such as Axxx he will probably hold up the ace for one round; when you come in with the king of spades, as is more than likely, you will be able to lead your second diamond and obtain a ruff. Then you will need just one further trick from somewhere to defeat the contract in neat fashion.

4. A forcing lead

You are said to play a FORCING game when your general plan is to weaken the declarer's trump holding. You do this by forcing him to ruff. You should always think about a forcing game when you hold four or more cards in the trump suit.

Game All. Dealer South.

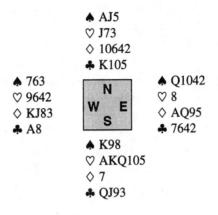

```
                    ♠ AJ5
                    ♡ J73
                    ◇ 10642
                    ♣ K105
   ♠ 763            ┌─────────┐        ♠ Q1042
   ♡ 9642           │    N    │        ♡ 8
   ◇ KJ83           │  W   E  │        ◇ AQ95
   ♣ A8             │    S    │        ♣ 7642
                    └─────────┘
                    ♠ K98
                    ♡ AKQ105
                    ◇ 7
                    ♣ QJ93
```

South	West	North	East
1♡	Pass	1NT	Pass
2♡	Pass	3♡	Pass
4♡	Pass	Pass	Pass

West might make a neutral lead such as the 7 of spades, but the fact that four trumps are held points to the lead of a low diamond. East wins and returns a diamond, which South has to ruff. Declarer plays off ace and king of hearts, because if the trumps are breaking 3-2 he will be able to draw trumps, force out the ace of clubs, and make ten easy tricks. When East discards a club on the second round of trumps, this vision fades.

The position will be:

```
                    ♠ AJ5
                    ♡ J
                    ◇ 106
                    ♣ K105
   ♠ 763            ┌─────────┐        ♠ Q1042
   ♡ 96             │    N    │        ♡ –
   ◇ KJ             │  W   E  │        ◇ Q9
   ♣ A8             │    S    │        ♣ 764
                    └─────────┘
                    ♠ K98
                    ♡ Q10
                    ◇ –
                    ♣ QJ93
```

South could draw trumps, but then would certainly lose a club and two diamonds. He may try a club in the diagram position, but West will win the second round and force again in diamonds. South should lose two more tricks however he plays.

5. Safety leads

Quite often the main concern of the opening leader will be not to give a trick away. Suppose that West holds:

♠ Q85
♡ 742
◇ A932
♣ K107

The bidding by his opponents goes:

South	North
1♡	2♡
2NT	3♡
4♡	Pass

This contract may be close, because South has gone to game without much encouragement from his partner. Sitting West, you have no clear choice between the side suits: any one of them might be brilliant or might be fatal. The natural play is to lead a trump and let the declarer do his own work.

From three small cards in a side suit it is usual to lead the top card, but there are occasions when a low card would be clearer. Suppose your partner has bid clubs or is at any rate known to hold length in the suit, and the actual distribution is:

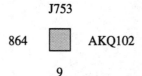

J753

864   AKQ102

9

If you lead the 8 and partner wins the first trick with the 10 it may not be clear to him that the next round will be ruffed by the declarer. This might not matter, but sometimes it might be very important for East to try another suit. On such occasions as this West should lead the lowest card, the 4. It will probably be clear to East that South could not hold three losers in the suit. As a matter of fact, some players, even when there is no special inference to be drawn about the distribution, habitually lead low from three small against a suit contract.

The Play by Third Hand

The majority of what we say here applies equally to the play in no trumps and in a suit contract. We look first at the play by third hand when partner has led a low card and dummy has low cards as well.

742

Q1065 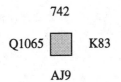 K83

AJ9

West leads the 5 and dummy plays low. Now every novice goes through the stage of withholding the king on the grounds (if any) that this might lead to decapitation by declarer's possible AQJ. That is infantile. As you can see, it costs a trick here because after the king has forced the ace the jack can be picked up by a lead from East on the next round. For East not to play the king on the first round is a horror known as 'finessing against partner'. There is nevertheless an important exception (bridge is like that):

82

J9753 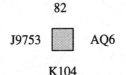 AQ6

K104

West leads the 5, dummy plays the 2; in a suit contract you would play the ace, but in no trumps the queen is a better card. The point is that if you part with the ace declarer will hold up the king until the third round, and your partner may have no quick entry.

Quite different are the occasions when you hold a card that can beat dummy's honour card.

Q75

J9862 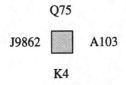 A103

K4

West leads the 6 and dummy plays the 7. To play the ace now would be disastrous – you must finesse the 10. Note that this wouldn't cost even if declarer held Jx or Jxx. There are innumerable situations of this kind, and quite often it is right to finesse against two of dummy's cards.

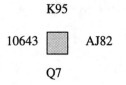

K95

10643　　AJ82

Q7

When West, at no trumps, leads the 3 and dummy plays the 5, East's best card is the 8. That's the only way to hold South to one trick in the suit.

Another stratagem that is often right for third hand is the unblock.

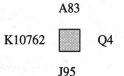

742

QJ1053　　K8

A95

West leads the queen. If you think for a moment, then play low, South may play you for a 'mug' and take the ace at once. You will feel a little foolish later when you are left in possession of the king.

This is a more tricky example of unblocking:

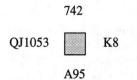

A83

K10762　　Q4

J95

West leads the 6 and South, who knows the position well enough, goes up with the ace in dummy. If you fail to unblock the queen there may be an ugly scene later!

Ducking Play

We have noted one or two occasions where either the declarer or a defender has declined to win a trick when he could easily have done so. The player is said to DUCK. A simple example for the defending side occurs when a suit is like this:

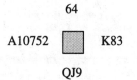

64

A10752　　K83

QJ9

West leads low to his partner's king and East returns the 8. When South plays the jack (or queen if it amuses him) West will duck, so that when next in the defenders will be able to run the remainder of the suit. If West had won the second trick and cleared the suit, and East had won the first trick for the defending side, there would have been a loss of communication.

The same kind of play is made very often by the attacking side.

K742

A63

If you hope to develop a long card don't play off ace, king and another: you duck the first or second round so that you keep better control.

Now that you see what is meant by ducking, let's see if you can follow an example which is not quite so simple.

♠ KQ852
♡ Q7
◊ 842
♣ A95

	♠ J94	N	♠ A106
	♡ J83	W E	♡ K964
	◊ J9753	S	◊ K10
	♣ Q8		♣ J632

♠ 63
♡ A1052
◊ AQ6
♣ K1074

South	West	North	East
1♣	Pass	1♠	Pass
1NT	Pass	2NT	Pass
3NT(i)	Pass	Pass	Pass

(i)   With 13 points and two 10s South is not minimum for the sequence he has followed and is entitled to accept the invitation to game.

West leads a low diamond to the king and it is natural for South to duck. He wins the next diamond with the ace and leads a spade to the king.

Now East may go wrong. If he takes the ace of spades and leads a club, say, it will be quite easy for South to establish the spades by playing queen and another. This will give him eight tricks and it won't be difficult to find a ninth. Neither defender can touch hearts without giving a trick away.

East would have done better to hold off the first round of spades. Then South would have lacked the entries to establish dummy's suit. And did it occur to you that South might have begun, not by leading a spade to the king, but by ducking the first round altogether? East would win and lead a club. South goes up with the king and plays a second spade. This way, he establishes the suit and still has the ace of clubs for entry.

Signals

A famous lady international, Rixi Markus, used to address her partners in these terms: 'Don't give me any signals. After a few tricks I will know what you've got better than you know yourself.' Where Rixi was concerned, that may have been true, but for the rest of the world an exchange of information by the defenders is absolutely essential.

Many signals are so familiar that one doesn't think of the play as in any sense convential. This is one example:

1075

J943   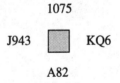   KQ6

A82

When West leads the 3 at some point an unskilful East may play the king. In a suit contract South might take the ace at once. Now if West comes in later he will think that South holds AQx and will fear to play a second round. If East had played the queen on the first round West would not have been so pessimistic. In other words, it is always right to *play* the lower, or lowest, of touching honours, although it is usually right to *lead* the highest. If ever you depart from this convention you must have your reasons.

Two important signals occur all the time in defence. First, a higher card than necessary may be played for two reasons.

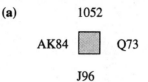

(a)   1052

AK84   [ ]   Q73

J96

When West leads the king in (a), East will signal encouragement by dropping the 7.

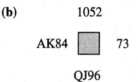

(b)   1052

AK84   [ ]   73

QJ96

It is the same in (b), though this time East looks forward to ruffing the third round. This high-low play is also called a PETER but the more modern word is ECHO.

Another way to signal is to drop the *lowest* card when you are not enthused.

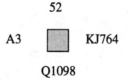

52

A3   [ ]   KJ764

Q1098

Perhaps East has opened or overcalled in this suit, or perhaps West is just being imaginative when he leads the ace. Unless he holds sure entries, East will discourage by dropping the 4.

Signals are used to show length as well as strength. Suppose that while declarer is playing a long suit you propose to discard from a different suit such as 8652: you show that you have an even number by playing high-low, perhaps the 6 and the 2. Don't think that since you have no important cards this is a waste of effort: your signal will help partner to count the hand and make the right discards himself.

Finally, when you hold a strong sequence and want to show this either on partner's lead or when following suit to an opponent, play the highest card you can afford.

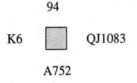

At some point in the play your partner, West, realises that the best hope for the defence is to attack this suit and advances the king. You don't have to look smug or even appreciative: just play the queen.

Quiz No. 6

1. What is the normal lead from sequences such as: KQJ, J109?

2. In a suit contract, what in the usual lead from an AK holding?

3. What is a forcing lead?

4. In a suit contract, what is the usual lead from three small, such as 752?

5. What is meant by a finesse against partner?

6. What is meant by a finesse against dummy?

7. When discarding, how do you show that you have an even number?

Answers to Quiz No. 6

1. Top of the sequence is normal; also top of a 'broken sequence' such as KQ10 or QJ9.

2. The king is traditional; from AK alone, the ace.

3. A lead whose general intent is to force the declarer to shorten his trumps by ruffing.

4. The standard lead is 'top of nothing', but when it will be plain to partner that only small cards are held the lowest card is right.

5. Suppose West leads low, dummy has three small, third hand such as KJ10; to play the 10, perhaps allowing South to win with the queen, would be a finesse against partner.

6. West leads low, dummy holds Qxx, and East A10x; now the 10 is a finesse against dummy, usually correct play.

7. By playing high-low with two middle cards.

DAY FIVE

5
MORE ABOUT BIDDING

Well, what's left? Quite a lot, actually, in the bidding field. Not much has been said about defensive and competitive bidding. When is it right to overcall? More important, when is it a mistake to overcall?

Defensive and Competitive Bidding

Even at the One level there is a difference in tactics between opening bids and simple overcalls. A player who opens the bidding with, say, One Club, is laying the groundwork for a possible game (or slam) contract. But a player who overcalls One Club with One Spade or One Heart may be thinking more about obstructing the opposition than reaching a good contract his way.

Of course, there are exceptions to that last remark. Second hand may hold two promising suits, for example, but as we shall see before long there are other ways in which a defender can introduce a strong hand.

Suppose that South opens the bidding, probably with One Heart or One Club, and West holds:

♠ KJ9643
♡ 4
♦ 10863
♣ A4

This would not be a sound opening bid, but it would be better than average overcall at the One level. Points are no longer the standard. What you need is to be well armed for the competitive battle that lies ahead.

Suppose, next, that South has opened One Club. What would you do sitting West with the following hands:

1. ♠ 64
    ♡ Q10642
    ◊ AJ74
    ♣ 62

Not a good overcall; the suit is poor and you are not shutting out any likely response.

2. ♠ 73
    ♡ Q2
    ◊ AK1085
    ♣ 9762

It probably wouldn't be fatal to overcall One Diamond, but partner will expect more and you will seldom achieve anything.

3. ♠ KJ985
    ♡ A76
    ◊ 1042
    ♣ 53

You would be on the weak side for a vulnerable overcall, but if not vulnerable you should probably hazard One Spade.

Now assume that the opening bid by South was One Heart. Sitting over him, you hold as West:

4. ♠ 63
    ♡ K10
    ◊ 7642
    ♣ AK1085

When you are thinking of an overcall at the Two level you are much more exposed to a penalty double, and vulnerability is important. This would be a poor overcall if you were vulnerable, and borderline if you were not.

5. ♠95
    ♡ K1086
    ◊ A4
    ♣ KQJ42

Not a bad hand in its way, but the fact that you are strong in the opponent's suit should incline you to pass. The affair may well turn out to your advantage.

6.   ♠ QJ5
      ♡ AQ3
      ◊ KQJ92
      ♣ 104

Now it is natural to overcall 1NT. If you were doubled it would be wise to retreat to Two Diamonds.

Jump Overcalls

A jump overcall, Two Spades or Three Clubs over One Diamond, is one of those calls that are differently interpreted by different players. Some would treat it as fairly strong, others as a defensive manoeuvre, a hand such as QJ10xxx with a side ace. If you have not discussed the matter with your partner, treat it as fairly strong; a good suit and 3 to $3\frac{1}{2}$ honour tricks.

Bidding in Fourth Position

You don't need a lot to reopen in fourth position when your opponents have died early.

South	West	North	East
1◊	Pass	1♠	Pass
2◊	Pass	Pass	?

You can be confident now that your partner has useful values. It would be sound tactics to reopen with a double (not a penalty double) or with Two Hearts on many hands that would not have justified intervention on the previous round. When it looks as though the two sides have about equal strength you must aim to push them up to the Three level at least. Competition of this sort is important; don't say to yourself 'They won't go far in Two Diamonds'.

Take-out Doubles and Redoubles

There is a very important area of the game which we have not examined yet. Suppose that One Diamond is opened on your right and you hold:

          ♠ KJ85
          ♡ Q6432
          ◊ 5
          ♣ AQ9

Your side might do very well in either of the major suits, but if you were to overcall either One Heart or One Spade you might find that you had picked the wrong one. You have what is called a TAKE-OUT double available which is quite different from the type of penalty double you have encountered so far. It shows that you have a fair hand, maybe a strong hand, and that you are interested to know what your partner holds. We will discuss this matter under various headings:

1. When is the double for take-out rather than for penalties?

2. What strength is needed in various situations?

3. What action is taken by the doubler's partner?

4. What action may be taken by the partner of the player who has been doubled?

5. What action may be taken by the player whose opening bid was doubled?

This is not, in fact, a difficult area of the game. In every case the action to be taken just depends on commonsense.

1. When is the double for take-out rather than for penalties?

There is a simple answer to this: any double at a low level (up to Three Diamonds in the tournament world) is for take-out when your partner has not made a positive call of any kind (if he has, you don't need to double to find where his strength lies). One or two examples:

(a)	South	West	North	East
	1◇	Pass	1♠	*Dble*

For take-out, with emphasis on the unbid suits.

(b)	South	West	North	East
	1♠	Dble	2♣	*Dble*

For penalties, because West has already given a picture of his hand.

(c)	South	West	North	East
	1◇	Pass	1♡	Pass
	1NT	Pass	2♡	*Dble*

For penalties; East could have doubled One Heart for take-out on the previous round. What has happened, no doubt, is that North has rebid a moderate six card suit and East sits over him with something like KJ10x in hearts and some other good cards.

(d)

South	West	North	East
1♡	Pass	1♠	Pass
2◇	Pass	Pass	*Dble*

This is neither a penalty double (East is on the wrong side of the diamonds) nor a take-out double, since the opponents have already named three suits. North, evidently, is weak and East is inviting partner to compete in any direction that appeals to him.

2. What strength is needed in various situations?

With favourable distribution – which means support for the three unnamed suits – the player in second position may double on, say, 11 points; not less, because there must be some standard on which partner can rely. In a sequence such as (d) above points are less important.

3. What action is taken by the doubler's partner?

More often than not, the responder to the double will simply bid his best suit at minimum level. If his only four-card suit is one called by the opposition he may have to respond in no trumps, but this should be avoided on bad hands. In addition, if partner's double of One Diamond comes round to you, and your only value is Qxxx of diamonds, you should prefer to bid your longer major rather than 1NT or pass the double. Never pass a take-out double unless you have strong trumps, not less than QJ1097.

When the responder to the double is fairly strong, 7 or 8 points upwards, he may give a jump response. This is not forcing. With a hand that looks like game opposite partner's double responder may bid the enemy suit.

(e)

South	West	North	East
1♡	Dble	Pass	2♡

East is saying: 'I have good values, probably enough for game. Let me hear from you.'

4. What action may be taken by the partner of the player who has been doubled?

As a rule, this player won't have much, but if he has a useful suit, something like KJ10xxx, he may name it. If he is fairly strong, about 8 points upwards, he may *redouble*, saying to partner, 'We have the balance of the cards, we may well be able to double them for penalties.' With support for partner in a weakish hand, raise his suit as freely as you dare.

5. What action may be taken by the player whose opening bid was doubled?

	(f)	South	West	North	East
		1 ◇	Dble	Pass	2 ♣
		Dble			

South is saying, 'I have a strong hand, not less than about 18 points; if you have anything we can double them.'

If you are not used to these sequences, you may think there's a lot to remember, but that's not so at all. The action to be taken, except perhaps in (e), is logical and plain.

Redouble for Rescue

There is a subtle difference between these two sequences:

1.	South	West	North	East
	1 ◇	2 ♣	Dble	*Redble*

West has been doubled for penalties. If he were happy about it East would pass. When he redoubles the inference is that he is void of clubs and would like his partner to move in some other direction (including diamonds).

2.	South	West	North	East
	1 ◇	Pass	Pass	Dble
	Redble			

South has not been doubled for penalties, so the redouble is not for rescue. He is saying to partner: 'I have a big hand, about 18 points upwards, so we may well have the balance of the cards. Double them if you can, on your next turn or later.'

Slam Bidding

As was mentioned earlier, there is a substantial bonus for bidding and making a small slam, 12 tricks, and a grand slam, 13 tricks. Grand slams are difficult to bid, even for the best players, and are not particularly well rewarded, because if you are one down in your grand slam the odds are that you will have surrendered the points for a small slam. The bonus for a small slam non-vulnerable is 500, vulnerable it is 750. This means that a slam on an even chance is just about worth bidding.

Sometimes – not very often in modern times – direct methods will be as good as any. Suppose East and West hold:

♠ A862		♠ KJ10753
♡ AK842		♡ 7
◇ 4		◇ AQ85
♣ KJ2		♣ Q6

The bidding begins:

West	**East**
1♡	1♠
3♠	4◇
?	

West will think: 'To make a slam try over Three Spades my partner must have good trumps and the ace of diamonds. My king of clubs is vital. Six spades!'

This contract will be laydown unless the spades are 3-0 and East begins with the 'wrong' top card.

Sometimes, too, it will soon become clear that there is a danger suit.

♠ J5		♠ Q73
♡ AJ105		♡ KQ8764
◇ AKQ1032		◇ J
♣ K		♣ AQ5

The bidding begins:

West	**East**
1◇	1♡
4♡	5♣
5◇	5♡
?	

This is a tricky hand in a way, because there are such good values in every suit but one. However, there is an easy escape from disaster through the use of CUEBIDDING. Over Four Hearts East shows a top control by making a cuebid of Five Clubs. West can do no less than cuebid in return with Five Diamonds. When East bids Five Hearts over this it is plain to West that the top spades are absent so he has no more to say.

Short suits – singletons and voids – are often just as valuable as aces and kings. On this hand West is bold enough to go beyond game because he has good controls.

♠ AQ852   ♠ K3
♡ K105   ♡ A74
◇ A852   ◇ KJ1064
♣ 3   ♣ J62

The bidding goes:

West	East
1♠	2◇
4◇	4♡
5♣	6◇
Pass	

West's Four Diamonds is perfectly sound. He has 'only 13' points, but the values are there. Then over Four Hearts he comes again with a cuebid in clubs, which is just what East wanted to hear.

As you might expect, the contract is not laydown: it will depend on not losing a trump trick. Here the odds are about 6 to 4 in your favour, and anything better than evens is reasonable.

Sometimes you will be able to calculate through the point count that you are in the slam zone. Suppose your partner opens 2NT and you have a balanced 13. Putting the two together you will have a minimum of 33, which should always provide a play for 6NT.

Blackwood Convention

As an aid to slam bidding there is the famous – or infamous – Blackwood convention. A bid of 4NT, when the agreed trump suit is clear at any rate to the player who makes the call, is an enquiry about aces. Partner then responds:

5♣	0 or 3 aces
5◇	1 or 4 aces
5♡	2 aces

A player who has bid 4NT, asking about aces, may follow with 5NT, to signify that all the aces are held.

The scheme works well on this type of hand where South opens one heart and North holds:

♠ 4
♡ KQ6
◇ AK10752
♣ KQ3

The bidding continues:

South	North
1♡	3◇
3♡	4NT
?	

This is sound use of Blackwood, because North will know what to do whether his partner shows one, two, or three aces.

Suppose, however, that North holds a slightly different hand:

♠ 4
♡ KQ6
◇ AKJ752
♣ QJ8

North is perhaps not worth his force of Three Diamonds, by modern standards, but in any event it would be a mistake to follow the same sequence as before. Suppose the response to 4NT is Five Hearts, denoting two aces: you won't know where you are: there might be two club losers and there might not. It is better here to respond Two Diamonds and give the partnership time to discover which suits are controlled, or just raise Three Hearts to Four Hearts.

Quiz No. 7

1. What is the meaning of a jump overcall, such as Two Hearts over an opponent's One Club opening?

2. How is a take-out double distinguished from a penalty double?

3. What do you need for a penalty pass of partner's take-out double?

4. One Heart on your left, double by partner, pass by third hand; what do you do with a hand strong enough for game?

Quiz No. 8

5. When is a redouble for rescue?

6. Approximately what odds are needed for a slam bid to be reasonable?

7. What is the meaning of a cuebid?

8. Responding to Blackwood, how do you show three aces?

Answers to Quiz No. 7

1. This is a matter of arrangement: either fairly strong, a good suit and between 3 and 4 honour tricks, or weak, a six card suit and not more than $1^1/2$ honour tricks.

2. At a low level a double is for take-out when partner has not named a suit or given some other indication of his holding.

3. A strong holding in the enemy suit, certain to win at least three or four tricks.

4. If you cannot make a direct game bid in any suit, bid Two Hearts, the enemy suit.

Answers to Quiz No. 8

5. When partner has been doubled for penalties at a low level.

6. About evens, either vulnerable or not.

7. A bid in a side suit whose object is to show a control; this may be either a high control, ace or king, or a low control, singleton or void.

8. By bidding Five Clubs, which is 0 or 3.

A NOTE ON THE LAWS AND PROPRIETIES

The International Laws of Contract Bridge, obtainable from stationers or from Victor Gollancz Ltd, or the English Bridge Union, have developed over a large number of years. They are extremely well set out but by no means easy to memorise. Any bridge club will have a copy and probably a tournament director who will be familiar with the Laws relating to the commonest irregularities such as Change of Call, Insufficient Bid, Dummy's Rights, Revoking (failure to follow suit) and suchlike.

More important, for beginners who are unlikely to be playing for stakes of any consequence, are the proprieties. Bridge is unplayable except on the basis that all bids and plays are made with no special emphasis and that no comment is made on partner's supposed inadequacies. Any special understanding between partners – any convention in bidding or play – must be explained to the opponents. Lastly, players are enjoined 'to maintain at all times a courteous attitude towards their partners and opponents'.

BRIDGE TERMS AND PHRASES

Above the line All scores other than those for tricks bid and made belong technically above the line across the centre of the score sheet

Balanced hand One that contains no singleton or void; usually one with 4-3-3-3, 4-4-3-2 or 5-3-3-2 distribution.

Below the line The score for tricks bid and made, such as 60 for Two Spades, is entered below the line.

Bid Strictly, a contract to make a given number of tricks in a specified call; used also as a general term to include Pass, Double and Redouble.

Blackwood A convention whereby a bid of 4NT asks partner to declare the number of aces he holds.

Call Any bid, Pass, Double, or Redouble.

Combination finesse A finesse where two adjacent cards are missing; used mostly when AJ10 is held.

Contract The final call of the auction, which is followed by three passes, establishes the level at which the hand will be played; may be One Club, may be 6NT doubled.

Control An ace (or void) is a first round control, a king (or singleton) a second round control.

Convention An agreement between partners to attach a special meaning to a call or play.

Cuebid	A bid that shows a control in a side suit, including the suit bid by the opponents.
Cut	The draw for partners, also the division of the pack before the deal.
Declarer	The player who first named the denomination in which the hand is due to be played and who handles dummy's cards as well as his own.
Defender	During the bidding, the side whose opponents opened the bidding; during the play, an opponent of the declarer.
Discard	When a player cannot follow suit and drops a card from another suit (not the trump suit) he is said to discard.
Double	Call that if passed out raises the stakes; see also Take-out Double.
Doubleton	The holding of two cards.
Duck	To play a low card for tactical reasons, when a higher card is available.
Dummy	The declarer's partner, who exposes his cards after the opening lead.
Endgame	Describes a critical situation towards the end of the play.
Entry	A card that affords access to a player's hand.
Exit	The play of a card that surrenders the lead.
Finesse	An attempt to win a trick, or establish a later trick, by leading towards a combination such as AQ or AJ10.
Follow suit	Play a card of the same suit as the one led.
Force	In the play, to lead a suit that the declarer can ruff, perhaps to his disadvantage; in the bidding, to make a call that forces partner to respond and will generally lead to game.

Game	A side that has scored 100 or more points below the line, in one or more ventures, has made a game.
Grand slam	A contract to win all thirteen tricks.
Hold up	Occurs when for tactical reasons a player declines to win a trick.
Honour	AKQJ10 are honour cards. A bonus is scored when four or five honours are held in the trump suit, or four aces at no trumps.
Jump	A jump raise, response, rebid, or overcall, is a bid (normally) one range higher than necessary.
Lead	The opening lead is made by the player on the left of the declarer. Subsequent leads are made by the player (including dummy) who won the preceding trick.
Major suit	Spades or hearts, counting 30 for each trick.
Minor suit	Diamonds or clubs, counting 20 for each trick.
No bid	Call with the same meaning as pass.
No trumps	Call in which all the suits are equal. No trumps score 40 below the line for the first trick, 30 for subsequent tricks.
Open	To make the first call; to make the first lead.
Overcall	Usually a bid by the defender on the opener's left.
Overruff	When partner or an opponent has ruffed, to ruff with a higher card.
Overtrick	A trick beyond the number for which declarer has contracted.
Partscore	A score below the line of less than 100, not enough for game unless added to a previous partscore.
Pass	Call signifying that the player is not making a positive call.
Penalty	Points scored above the line when a contract has been defeated.

Penalty double	A double intended to penalise the opponents, as opposed to a take-out double.
Penalty pass	This occurs when the partner of a player who has made a take-out double passes because he is strong in the suit that has been doubled.
Peter	The play of two cards in descending order to show a doubleton or to express encouragement.
Point count	A method of valuation in which points are assigned to high cards.
Pre-empt	To make a high call that will leave the opponents little room in which to exchange information.
Protect	To reopen the bidding after two passes in case partner has undisclosed values.
Raise	To express support for partner's call.
Redouble	When a side has been doubled, either player may redouble to express confidence; in some situations the redouble may have the opposite sense, proposing escape from the present contract.
Reverse	When a player who has opened with a bid of One follows with a bid of Two in a higher suit, such as One Diamond followed by Two Hearts, he is said to reverse, a sign of strength.
Revoke	A player who fails to follow suit when able to do so commits a revoke and is subject to penalty.
Rubber	A side that wins two games has won the rubber. Then a new contest begins.
Ruff	To play a trump when a side suit has been led.
Sacrifice	To contest with a bid that is likely to be doubled and defeated.
Sequence	Three or more consecutive cards in a suit. QJ9 is a broken sequence, Q109 an inner sequence.

Side suit	A suit other than the trump suit.
Sign-off	A bid that denies additional values.
Simple	A simple raise, response etcetera is one made at minimum level.
Single raise	Support for partner's call that raises the bidding by only one stage.
Singleton	The holding of one card in a suit.
Small slam	A contract to win twelve tricks.
Take-out double	A double that shows strength and asks partner to express his holding.
Trial bid	A bid of a non-genuine suit, a try for game.
Trick	The play of four cards, one by each player, forms a trick.
Trump	The suit in which a contract is played; a card of this suit; to play a card that has superior rank to a card of any other suit.
Unblock	To play or discard a card that might otherwise obstruct the run of a suit or win an unwanted trick.
Vulnerable	A side that has won a game in an unfinished rubber becomes vulnerable; thereafter penalties, also bonuses in a doubled or redoubled contract, or for a slam contract, are increased.

INDEX

**Most entries refer to the first occasion
on which a term or subject is mentioned**

SCORING TABLE

Score below the line for tricks (beyond six) bid and made:

Diamonds or clubs	20 per trick
Spades or hearts	30 per trick
No trumps	40 for the first trick, 30 for each additional trick

Multiply by 2 if doubled, by 4 if redoubled

100 points wins game, but no separate score is recorded until the bonus for rubber is added.

Score above the line:

	Overtricks	
	Not Vulnerable	*Vulnerable*
Undoubled	Trick Value	Trick Value
Doubled	100 per trick	200 per trick
Redoubled	200 per trick	400 per trick
Bonus for making any DOUBLED CONTRACT 50 Bonus for making any REDOUBLED CONTRACT 100		

Honours

Scored by either side: Four honours in the trump suit held in one hand – 100; Five honours – 150
Four aces in one hand at no trumps –150

Slams

	Not Vulnerable	Vulnerable
Small Slam (six)	500	750
Grand Slam (seven)	1000	1500

Penalties for Undertricks

Contract	Not Vulnerable			Vulnerable		
number of tricks down	Undoubled	Doubled	Red'bled	Undoubled	Doubled	Red'bled
1	50	100	200	100	200	400
2	100	300	600	200	500	1000
3	150	500	1000	300	800	1600
4	200	800	1600	400	1100	2200
5 etc	50 for each extra trick	300 for each extra trick	600 for each extra trick	100 for each extra trick	300 for each extra trick	600 for each extra trick

Rubber Bonus

For rubber won in two games: 700
For rubber won in three games: 500

Unfinished Rubber

Bonus for a side that is game up: 300
Bonus for a partscore in an unfinished game: 50

Settlement

It is usual, at rubber bridge, to play for 'so much' a 100. When the difference is, for example, 950, this is counted as 10 points.

Specimen Rubber

WE	THEY
60(4) 30(1)	700(5) 500(3)
60(1)	150(2)
40(4)	120(5)
190	1470

(1) WE play 2♡ and make 3.

(2) THEY play 4♠ and make 5; technically 120 below and 30 above, but the full amount is always entered below.

(3) WE go three down in 3NT doubled, 500 away.

(4) WE play 1NT, make 3; 40 below 60 above.

(5) THEY play 4♡, just made. Rubber in two games: 700.

13 points to THEM; *bien joué!*